KINGDOM PERCEPTION

Developing Accurate Understanding Of Kingdom Principles

Emmanuel Echidime

Table of Contents

Acknowledgement

I am so thankful to Almighty God who by His infinite mercy has allowed me to gain knowledge and revelation into His word and to pen this into a book.

I want to acknowledge my mother, Margret Echidime, who taught me from a young age to trust and depend on God for everything.

My brothers Anthony and Joseph, and my sisters Grace and Patience, who showed me unconditional love throughout my early years, and especially for their support during my transition out of Nigeria.

To the leaders of New Life Global Church for their prayers and support both personally and within the ministry as I embarked on this endeavor.

To Bishop Pat Johnson, the founder and general overseer of Canadian Christian Ministries for his role within my life and the contribution he made towards the establishment of New Life Global Church.

To my wife, Pastor Sondra Echidime and our children who stood by me during the planting of New Life Global Church and all the challenges that we faced during this time and through to the writing of this book. I want to thank you for managing our household for many hours on your own while I devoted time to complete this book. May the Lord Almighty bless and reward you for your act of love.

Finally, to my spiritual Father, Apostle Israel Onoriobe, I cannot thank you enough for your mentorship and friendship. It is through your mentorship and persuasion, as well as your encouragement and assistance that this book is available today. May the Lord Almighty continue to bless you as you take His word to the nations of the world.

I am convinced *and* confident of this very thing, that He who has begun a good work in you will [continue to] perfect *and* complete it until the day of Christ Jesus [the time of His return] - Philippians 1:6 (Amplified Bible).

Foreword One

"Kingdom Perception" is valuable tool for anyone involved in ministry, especially those involved in pastoral, teaching, evangelical, missionary and discipleship ministry. For most of us perception is reality. The way we perceive things determine our actions hence our destiny. Perception determines the way we approach business, church, family and issues affecting our daily lives. It also has a strong influence in the way we relate to people.

The church is made up of people. The people are a part of a Kingdom. How we deal with people will determine whether they enter the Kingdom, remain in the Kingdom or leave the Kingdom. The right knowledge of the Kingdom of God is essential for ensuring people live as the King intends them to live in His Kingdom. Therefore, we must propagate ministry from God's viewpoint.

This book "Kingdom Perception" written by Apostle Emmanuel Echidime gives a clear and accurate understanding of the correct perception of the Kingdom of God. It tells about our King, His domain, the citizens and the principles that govern His Kingdom. When you understand the Kingdom and how it operates, it will usher you into the level of ministry as the Apostles and the Prophets in the New Testament.

I therefore recommend this book to believers of all denominations for use in preaching, Bible studies, seminars, libraries, Bible colleges and seminaries, because the way we perceive the Kingdom will determine our success or failure and our ultimate destiny.

Foreword by:

Bishop Pat Maxwell A. Johnson
General Overseer and Administrative Bishop:
Canadian Christian Ministries (CCM).
Oshawa, Ontario, Canada

Foreword Two

One of the greatest hindrances to the understanding and development of Kingdom patterns and principles affecting our walk with the Lord is our "mindset".

Wrong perception affects the effectiveness of true Kingdom lifestyle and the principles of Christological patterns.

Wrong perception affects the recognition and fulfilment of our true purpose and robs us of our identity in Christ.

Wrong perception disempowers the Church from her true authority and sphere of influence.

Wrong perception will rob us of our inheritance in Christ.

<u>The greatest part of our Christian walk is the realignment of our thoughts [perception] to the will of Christ and His Kingdom, because accurate thinking of the Kingdom will produce an effective accurate lifestyle and fulfilment of purpose.</u>

With these thoughts, I highly recommend this book "Kingdom Perception" and the ministry of Apostle Emmanuel Echidime. I believe it will empower the Church and awaken within us the awareness of our true purpose and the reality of fulfilment and freedom in Christ and His Kingdom.

I have had the privilege of living and discipling Apostle Emmanuel Echidime, his family and his local assembly (New Life Global Church) in Oshawa, Ontario, Canada regarding apostolic concepts and some of the things pertaining to the Kingdom of God. We have all travelled and ministered together in the nations. It is my joy to see his progress and walk in present truth of Christ and His Kingdom.

I pray that the Lord will give you greater understanding and accurate perception of His Kingdom and purposes as you read this book.

Yours in His Kingdom,

Apostle Israel Onoriobe
World Vision Crusade Outreach Ministries
Cape Town – South Africa
www.wvcom-international.org

Chapter 1

Kingdom Perception

Perception is defined as the ability to see, hear or become aware of something through the senses. It is a way of knowing, understanding and interpreting something.

As the body of Christ, we must have a clear and accurate perception of the kingdom of God, because we are living in a religious world full of different interpretations of the kingdom of God, but void of the original intent of God's mind and purpose.

To have the right perception of the kingdom of God, there is a great need for us to return to God's original intent, plan and purpose for His kingdom, without which we will misinterpret His kingdom and misconstrue His purpose.

".... it's important to look at things from God's point of view...." – 1 Corinthians 4:6 **Message Bible.**

The Hebrew word for "kingdom" is "mamlakah," which means sovereignty, dominion, reign or a realm.

The Greek word for "kingdom" is the word "basileia," which means kingship, sovereignty, authority and rule.

Both definitions speak of the reign and the rule of God, both in the world (the earthly realm), and in the heart of men.

A kingdom is a realm over which a king exercises his authority and dominion. <u>Jesus Christ is the King over the kingdom of God, and the realm of His kingdom includes both the heavens and the earth. It is important to note that King Jesus rules and reigns over all the heavens and the earth.</u> This means that whenever we speak about the kingdom of God, our understanding must not be limited to just the heavens, but the earth must be inclusive as well.

However, our understanding must not be limited to a place, because the kingdom of God is not just about a place, but more about the sovereign rule and reign of God within, and amid men.

"And when He was demanded of the Pharisees, when the kingdom of God should come, He answered them and said, the kingdom of God cometh not with observation: Neither shall they say, Lo here! or, lo there! for, <u>behold, the kingdom of God is within you</u>" – Luke 17:20-21.

The Pharisees ask Jesus a very significant question about the coming of the kingdom of God. His response makes us to understand that the kingdom of God is not about a place, but about the rule and reign of God within the hearts of men. Jesus didn't respond and say, the kingdom of God is a place [in heaven where we are flying to inherit], but rather he said the kingdom of God is a sovereign rule and reign of God within the hearts of men, which is a present reality. The kingdom is here, and it is progressively advancing and influencing both the hearts of men and the world.

It is the misconception of the kingdom that makes people think it is something yet to come, when it is already here [as a present reality among us]. <u>Jesus said, the kingdom of God is within and among us</u>. We are not waiting for the kingdom; we are living in the kingdom. The kingdom of God is a present reality, and it is progressive until its culmination at Christ's return. However, religion tells us otherwise; that is why so many people are living their lives the way they do, and hoping to fly to the kingdom someday.

If we carefully study the scriptures, we would understand that Jesus preached only one message, which is the kingdom of God. The kingdom of God was also the central theme of Jesus' mission.

"From that time Jesus began to preach, and to say, repent: for the kingdom of heaven is at hand" - Matthew 4:17.

"And Jesus went about all Galilee, teaching in their synagogues, and <u>preaching the gospel of the kingdom,</u> and healing all manner of sickness and all manner of disease among the people." - Matthew 4:23.

"And Jesus went about all the cities and villages, teaching in their synagogues, and <u>preaching the gospel of the kingdom,</u> and healing every sickness and every disease among the people." - Matthew 9:35.

"Now after that John was put in prison, Jesus came into Galilee, <u>preaching the gospel of the kingdom of God,</u> and saying, the time is fulfilled, and <u>the kingdom of God is at hand</u>: repent ye, and believe the gospel." - Mark 1:14-15.

".... and the people sought him, and came unto him, and stayed him, that he should not depart from them. And he said unto them, <u>I must preach the kingdom of God</u> to other cities also: <u>for therefore am I sent</u>." - Luke 4:42-43.

In this 21st century, the message of Jesus Christ has not changed. When we read the scriptures we will understand that the only message that Jesus commanded His disciples (known as the apostles) to preach was the message of the kingdom of God.

"Then He called His twelve disciples together, and gave them power and authority over all devils, and to cure diseases. And <u>He sent them to preach the kingdom of God,</u> and to heal the sick." - Luke 9:1-2.

"And He said unto them, Go ye into all the world, and preach the gospel to every creature" – Mark 16:15.

In other words, what was given to us to preach is nothing but the gospel of the kingdom of God. The ability to see beyond the physical realm and see the spiritual is a vital instrument in having the right perception as we understand the kingdom and embrace this reality. Understanding the kingdom reality will ultimately affect the way we live and how we deal with people.

In addition, having the right perception of the kingdom will make us so mindful of the kingdom and all that pertains to it, rather than just the riches of this earthly world.

Jesus said the kingdom of God must be *'received'* and accepted before we can enter it. In other words, it is necessary to receive the kingdom of God as a present reality right now.

In order for us to fully enjoy the benefits of the kingdom, we must have the right perception of the Kingdom. OUR PERCEPTION OF THE KINGDOM WILL DETERMINE HOW WE SEE, RECEIVE AND ENTER IT.

Taking the Kingdom:

"And from the days of John the Baptist until now the kingdom of heaven suffereth violence, and the violent take it by force" – Matthew 11:12.

John the Baptist was a forerunner of the message of the kingdom (Matthew 3:1-3). God had chosen him to break the 430 years of divine silence that had existed since the prophet Malachi. John was the Spirit-anointed bridge from the Old Covenant to the New Covenant. John was the last of the Old Testament prophets and stood on the point of a new dispensation. His preaching was the end of the Law and the beginning of the Promise of Grace. From the time John preached his message until this very day the kingdom of heaven is being taken by those who are pressing into it.

"There was a man of the Pharisees, named Nicodemus, a ruler of the Jews: The same came to Jesus by night, and said unto him, Rabbi, we know that thou art a teacher come from God: for no man can do these miracles that thou doest, except God be with him. <u>Jesus answered and said unto him, Verily, verily, I say unto thee, except a man be born again, he cannot see the kingdom of God</u>. Nicodemus saith unto him, how can a man be born when he is old? can he enter the second time into his mother's womb, and be born? <u>Jesus answered, Verily, verily, I say unto thee, except a man be born of water and of the Spirit, he cannot enter into the kingdom of God</u>"- John 3:1-5.

Jesus Christ [The King of the Kingdom] in His conversation with Nicodemus [a ruler of the Jewish Council] regarding the New Birth, made some bold statements which reveals an important principle regarding the Kingdom of God. This revelation from Jesus makes us to understand that the kingdom of God can be 'seen' and 'entered' into.

"Seeing the Kingdom," means to "know, be acquainted and to experience it." It also has a root word in the Greek, which means, 'a watching from a distance.'

"Entering the Kingdom," means to "to come in, to possess and fully walk in the reality of God's will, domain and authority (both NOW and in the age to come)."

"Seeing" and "Entering" the kingdom of God are two different dimensions of experience with the kingdom.

To "Enter the Kingdom" requires us first to receive the Kingdom, because we are receiving a kingdom that cannot be moved.

"Wherefore we receiving a kingdom which cannot be moved, let us have grace, whereby we may serve God acceptably with reverence and godly fear" - Hebrews 12:28.

Jesus said, the Kingdom of God must be *'received'* before we can enter it. In other words, it is necessary to receive the kingdom of God as a present reality right now.

The Greek word for "Receiving" is "dechomai," which means, "to take," "to accept," or "to welcome."

"Truly I tell you, whoever does not receive and accept and welcome the kingdom of God like a little child [does] positively shall not enter it at all" – Mark 10:13-15 Amplified Bible.

Therefore, the order is to 'See', 'Receive' and 'Enter,' is how we press into the kingdom to take it.

Our wrong perception of the kingdom is a hindrance to us receiving the kingdom. This was why the Jews did not receive Jesus Christ as their Messiah - their perception of Him.

"And you have not His word (His thought) living in your hearts, because you do not believe and adhere to and trust in and rely on Him Whom He has sent. [That is why you do not keep His message living in you, because you do not believe in the Messenger Whom He has sent.] You search and investigate and pore over the Scriptures diligently, because you suppose and trust that you have eternal life through them. And these [very Scriptures] testify about Me! And still you are not willing [but refuse] to come to Me, so that you might have life" – John 5:38-40 Amplified Bible.

Their perception about Christ is that He is the son of a carpenter and not the Messiah; because of this, they missed the Messiah entirely who was present among them.

The Jews rejected Jesus Christ because of their perception of the Messiah; He failed to do what they thought their Messiah would do. They expected Him to destroy all of their enemies and establish a physical kingdom in Israel with Jerusalem as their capital, which would become a prominent nation of the world – [even until this day, the

Jewish nation do not believe or receive Jesus Christ as the Messiah].

According to Isaiah 53 and (other related scriptures), the prophecy about the coming Messiah did not only speak of a glorious and magnificent Messiah, but it also described a suffering Messiah who would be persecuted and killed by His people to bring salvation to them. However, the Jews chose to focus only on prophesies that discussed his glorious victories, and not His suffering and crucifixion that would bring the redemption. All they thought, believed and expected was the Messiah that would come and deliver them from the bondage of the Roman Empire and set up His kingdom, and they become the rulers.

Jesus said to them that He was the Messiah, but their perception of Who He was, made them reject Him. Their minds were convinced that He was not the Messiah. Jesus said, *'the Father who sent Me has Himself testified about Me'* – John 5:37a.

Basic Concepts of the Kingdom:

It is important that we have the right perception of Christ and His Kingdom, as this will ultimately affect every aspect of our lives – our spiritual identity, how we approach Him, how we relate with Him and how we lead in our service for Him.

There are four basic concepts we must understand which govern the principle of a kingdom:

1. The King
2. The Domain
3. The Citizens
4. The Law

The King: Every kingdom is governed by a king, and everything regarding the kingdom revolves around the king. Without the king, there is NO kingdom.

Power and authority does not belong to the people, but to the king. A kingdom does not operate a democratic system of government, but a theocratic rule. God's kingdom is a THEOCRATIC government with an ABSOLUTE RULE; and His rule is that of love, justice, truth, peace, equity and righteousness.

Jesus Christ is the King of the Kingdom of God, and everything regarding God's purpose and will is centered around Him. He reigns over ALL things.

Isaiah 9:6-7, Hebrews 1:8, 1 Corinthians 15:25-28, Psalm 89:14.

The Domain: A domain is the territory owned or controlled by a ruler or government. Every kingdom has a specified sphere of dominion, so it is important to note that the domain of the kingdom of God that Christ [The King] rules over is inclusive of the heavens, the earth and beneath the earth. Therefore, when we hear the word, our mind must not be limited to think only of heaven. We must broaden our understanding to know that God's will and purpose is inclusive of the heavens and the earth. Therefore, we were admonished to pray in this manner, **"Thy Kingdom Come and *Thy Will Be Done on Earth as It Is in Heaven" – Matthew* 6:10.**

Psalms 24:1, Isaiah 66:1.

The Citizens: Every kingdom has subjects whom the king rules over. They are the people or citizens of the kingdom. God has translated those who believe in Christ Jesus into the kingdom of His Dear Son [Jesus Christ]. They are the citizens of the kingdom of God.

The Church of the Lord Jesus Christ is the body of community of people that form the citizens of the Kingdom of God.

Colossians 1:3, Philippians 3:20, Ephesians 2:19, 1 Peter 2:9-10.

The Law: The law is a system of rules recognized as a legal constitution, which regulates the actions of its citizens, enforced by its government.

The eternal word of God is the very essence of truth and the righteous law, which regulates God's kingdom. [It is the governing principles by which Christ rules His kingdom]. The Word of God must become the ONLY measuring standard by which our lives be governed, as we subject ourselves as citizens of God's kingdom. Obedience is important and necessary as we observe all that is written therein in His word – The Law of life and the legal constitution of God's kingdom.

Psalms 119:89, Psalm 119:160, Psalm 147:19.

Chapter 2

Knowing Your Spiritual Identity

It is vital for us, as believers in Christ Jesus, to have an accurate perception of our spiritual identity in Christ, and of His Kingdom. We need to know and understand who we are in Christ Jesus in order for us to live an effective kingdom life.

The most significant revelation we can receive from God is to know and understand who we are in Christ. This will greatly determine our fruitfulness and success in all we do towards the fulfilment of His divine purpose for our lives. When we know our identity in relation to Christ, it will change the way we live and cause us to rise above adversity, mediocrity and ignorance that can easily beset us in our walk with the Lord. Not having a full understanding of our identity in Him will keep us immature and living far below our rights and privileges in Christ as His children.

"Now what I mean [when I talk about children and their guardians] is this: as long as the heir is a child, he does not differ at all from a slave even though he is the [future owner and] master of all [the estate]; but he is under [the authority of] guardians and household administrators or managers until the date set by his

father [when he is of legal age]. So also, we [whether Jews or Gentiles], when we were children (spiritually immature), were kept like slaves under the elementary [man-made religious or philosophical] teachings of the world. But when [in God's plan] the proper time had fully come, God sent His Son, born of a woman, born under the [regulations of the] Law, so that He might redeem and liberate those who were under the Law, that we [who believe] might be adopted as sons [as God's children with all rights as fully grown members of a family]. And because you [really] are [His] sons, God has sent the Spirit of His Son into our hearts, crying out, [a]"Abba! Father!". Therefore, you are no longer a slave (bond-servant), but a son; and if a son, then also an heir through [the gracious act of] God [through Christ]. But at that time, when you did not know [the true] God and were unacquainted with Him, you [Gentiles] were slaves to those [pagan] things which by [their very] nature were not and could not be gods at all. Now, however, since you have come to know [the true] God [through personal experience], or rather to be known by God, how is it that you are turning back again to the weak and worthless elemental principles [of religions and philosophies], to which you want to be enslaved all over again?" – Galatians 4:1-9 Amplified Bible.

The scripture makes it clear that though we are sons [having the full right of ownership of our father's wealth], yet, because we are spiritually immature and ignorant, we are just like slaves with no entitlement, until we mature to the fullness of His will and purpose in our sonship in Him. This is only possible through the full and accurate knowledge of our Lord Jesus Christ, who has begotten us through His blood.

Paul the apostle prayed a very significant prayer for the believers in Ephesus when he first heard of their faith in the Lord Jesus Christ. He prayed for the spiritual eyes of their heart to have a greater revelation, knowledge and understanding through the Holy Spirit, and in doing so that they will know Christ, and this knowing will bring them into the understanding of their calling and inheritance in Christ. Having the right perception of who we are in Christ will ultimately motivate us to want to have all that has been given to us in Christ Jesus.

"[I always pray] that the God of our Lord Jesus Christ, the Father of glory, may grant you a spirit of wisdom and of revelation [that gives you a deep and personal and intimate insight] into the true knowledge of Him [for we know the Father through the Son]. And [I pray] that the eyes of your heart [the very center and core of your being] may be enlightened [flooded with light by the Holy Spirit], so that you will know and cherish the hope [the divine guarantee, the confident expectation] to which He has called you, the riches of His glorious inheritance in the saints (God's people), and [so that you will begin to know] what the immeasurable and unlimited and surpassing greatness of His [active, spiritual] power is in us who believe. These are in accordance with the working of His mighty

strength which He produced in Christ when He raised Him from the dead and seated Him at His own right hand in the heavenly places, far above all rule and authority and power and dominion [whether angelic or human], and [far above] every name that is named [above every title that can be conferred], not only in this age and world but also in the one to come. And He put all things [in every realm] in subjection under Christ's feet, and appointed Him as [supreme and authoritative] head over all things in the church, which is His body, the fullness of Him who fills and completes all things in all [believers]" – Ephesians 1:17-23 Amplified Bible.

Religion and the traditions of men have taught us to think that we must do certain things to appease God in order for Him to bless us or to make Him love us. We may think it is the greater work we do for God that will bring His love to us, but that is a lie. Having the right perception of who we are in Christ helps us to understand and to know that those things have already been accomplished in Christ Jesus.

"Blessed and worthy of praise be the God and Father of our Lord Jesus Christ, who has blessed us with every spiritual blessing in the heavenly realms in Christ" - Ephesians 1:3 Amplified Bible.

It is NOT what we do, but what Christ has done. This is what Grace is all about. The word of God says He has blessed us [past tense, *not* will bless us or may bless us] when we do something for Him. He (Christ) has already done it – it is a done deal. All that is left for us is to believe in the finished work of Christ and receive it by faith.

When we have an accurate perception and understanding of who we are in Christ, it will help us tremendously to live our lives as God intends for us. It will bring fulfilment of our true purpose and destiny in Christ.

The truth is that when we come into agreement with who God says we are, our lives will begin to reflect His will and purpose for us. The more we come into agreement with God's word about our identity in Him (Christ), the more our behavior will begin to reflect our GOD-GIVEN identity.

It is my desire to see the people of God taking their position as the sons of God in fulfilling their purpose and destiny in Christ.

We must embrace the truth that it is only God's opinion that matters in our lives. We must accept what God says about us and come into agreement with Him and His word. It is through accepting this truth concerning us that we become the spiritual person He has desired for us to be.

Understanding who we are in Christ will constitute a strong foundation on which we can build our lives upon. Therefore, constantly renewing our minds is imperative to the knowledge of who we are in Christ, which is the key to a successful and fulfilled Christian life. When we do this, we will be transformed and progressively changed, and not be conformed to the patterns and systems of this world, as we spiritually mature.

"Do not be conformed to this world, but continually be transformed by the renewing of your minds so that you may be able to determine what God's will is—what is proper, pleasing, and perfect [in His plan and purpose for you]" – Romans 12:2 ISV – [Emphasis is mine].

So many of us have allowed the opinions of people to form our spiritual identity, and by so doing we are living our lives based on what people are saying and thinking of us. This is very wrong and unacceptable as a child of God. We are more than the perception of men. We are who God says we are!

Your identity doesn't depend on something you do or have done or what people say. Again, your identity is *who God says you are!*

When you give your life to the Lord Jesus Christ you become a new creation - the old you has passed away and you are now a new creature in Him.

"Therefore, if anyone is in Christ [that is, grafted in, joined to Him by faith in Him as Savior], he is a new creature [reborn and renewed by the Holy Spirit]; the old things [the previous moral and spiritual condition] have passed away. Behold, new things have come [because

spiritual awakening brings a new life]" – 2 Corinthians 5:17 Amplified Bible.

In Christ Jesus, there is a spiritual awakening – the revelation of the resurrection of the newness of life (spiritual identity) that you now possess in Him. You are no longer the old person you used to be. You are now recreated and restored to the fulness of the image of God in your spirit. Therefore, there is a need for you to start living from your new person, *and not the old man.*

"But to as many as did receive and welcome Him, He gave the right [the authority, the privilege] to become children of God, that is, to those who believe in (adhere to, trust in, and rely on) His name - who were born, not of blood [natural conception], nor of the will of the flesh [physical impulse], nor of the will of man [that of a natural father], but of God [that is, a divine and supernatural birth - they are born of God - spiritually transformed, renewed, sanctified]" – John 1:12-13 Amplified Bible.

We need to constantly study the scriptures to find out who we are in Christ and what God has said about us, so we can come into agreement with Him and His word.

Because you are in Christ, EVERY ONE of these statements is true of you:

You have been redeemed from the penalty of sin.

"In whom we have redemption [because of His sacrifice, resulting in] the forgiveness of our sins [and the cancellation of sins' penalty]" – Colossians 1:14 Amplified Bible.

You are accepted; you are no longer an outcast.

"To the praise of the glory of His grace, by which He made us accepted in the Beloved" – Ephesians 1:6 Amplified Bible.

Is it not awesome to know that we are no longer a stranger in the kingdom of our Father? We are SONS. Hallelujah!

You are a joint heir with Jesus, sharing His inheritance with Him.

"And if [we are His] children, [then we are His] heirs also: heirs of God and fellow heirs with Christ [sharing His spiritual blessing and inheritance], if indeed we share in His suffering so that we may also share in His glory" – Romans 8:17 Amplified Bible.

You are united with God and have one spirit with Him.

"But the one who is united and joined to the Lord is one spirit with Him" – 1 Corinthians 6:17.

It is imperative to know that NOW that you are a new creation in Christ, you have oneness with the spirit of God. Yes, you have the spirit of God living in you.

When you were born again, the Spirit of God instantly regenerated your spirit. In fact, it was your spirit that was instantly born again [but you soul (your mind, will and emotions) is progressively being renewed and transformed – Romans 12:2]. Your body experiences the fullness of immortality at the climax of the age, because death is defeated. So yes, you have the Spirit of God in you.

You are free from condemnation.

"Therefore, there is now no condemnation [no guilty verdict, no punishment] for those who are in Christ Jesus [who believe in Him as personal Lord and Savior]. For the law of the Spirit of life [which is] in Christ Jesus [the law of our new being] has set you free from the law of sin and of death" **– Romans 8:1 Amplified Bible.**

It is heart breaking to see the people of God living in ignorance and the lies of the enemy. They fail to understand that the judgement and the guilt of their sins have been put upon Jesus, so they can experience true freedom in Him – Isaiah 53:4, Romans 8:1.

Your sins have been paid for by the sacrifice of His blood on the cross. You have been forgiven. God is not counting your sins against you – 2 Corinthians 5:19.

We must stop believing in the lies of the enemy that tell us that we are not good enough to receive the blessings of God, and that we cannot be used by God because of our past mistakes and our way of living. We must understand that through Christ Jesus we have been qualified to receive all that heaven has to offer.

You are the temple of God. His Spirit and His life lives in you.

"Do you not know that your body is a temple of the Holy Spirit who is within you, whom you have [received as a gift] from God, and that you are not your own [property]?" – 1 Corinthians 6:19.

<u>*You are complete in Jesus Christ. Yes, you DO NOT need anybody to complete you in Christ. You are already complete in Him. Praise God.*</u>

"For in Him all the fullness of Deity (the Godhead) dwells in bodily form [completely expressing the divine essence of God]. And in Him you have been made complete [achieving spiritual stature through Christ], and He is the head over all rule and authority [of every angelic and earthly power] – Colossians 2:9-10.

Yes, you are complete in Him and the fullness of Christ abides in you. Therefore, you do not need people or things to make you complete. You must have this revelation and understanding ingrained in you.

You are a new creation because you are in Christ.

"Whoever is a believer in Christ is a new creation. The old way of living has disappeared. A new way of living has come into existence" – 2 Corinthians 5:17 GW.

You are chosen of God, holy and dearly loved – God loves you and has chosen you as His own special one.

"But you are A CHOSEN RACE, A royal PRIESTHOOD, A CONSECRATED NATION, A [special] PEOPLE FOR God's OWN POSSESSION, so that you may proclaim the excellencies [the wonderful deeds and virtues and perfections] of Him who called you out of darkness into His marvelous light" – 1 Peter 2:9 Amplified Bible.

You are established, anointed, and sealed by God.

"Now it is God who establishes and confirms us [in joint fellowship] with you in Christ, and who has anointed us [empowering us with the gifts of the Spirit]" – 2 Corinthians 1:21 Amplified Bible.

You do not have the spirit of fear. God has given you the Spirit of love, power, and a sound mind.

"For God hath not given us the spirit of fear; but of power, and of love, and of a sound mind [abilities that result in a calm, well-balanced mind and self-control]" – 2 Timothy 1:7 [Emphasis is mine].

You are God's co-worker.

"We are God's co-workers. You are God's field. You are God's building" – 1 Corinthians 3:9 GW.

You are seated in heavenly places with Christ.

"And He raised us up together with Him [when we believed], and seated us with Him in the heavenly places, [because we are] in Christ Jesus: – Ephesians 2:6 Amplified Bible.

You are blessed with all spiritual blessings in heavenly places.

"Praise the God and Father of our Lord Jesus Christ! Through Christ, God has blessed us with every spiritual blessing that heaven has to offer" – Ephesians 1:3 GW.

You have a direct access to the Father (God).

"For through Him we both have access in one Spirit to the Father" – Ephesians. 2:18 ESV.

You have been chosen to bear and produce fruit.

"You have not chosen me, but I have chosen you. I have appointed you to go and produce fruit that will last, so that whatever you ask the Father in my name, he will give it to you" – John. 15:16 ISV.

You are one of God's living stones, being built up in Christ as a spiritual house.

"Ye also, as living stones, are built up a spiritual house, to be a holy priesthood, to offer up spiritual sacrifices, acceptable to God through Jesus Christ" – 1 Peter 2:5 ASV.

You have been given exceeding great and precious promises by God to share in His divine nature.

"Whereby.... [you have been given] exceeding great and precious promises: that by these ye might be partakers of the divine nature, having escaped the corruption that is in the world through lust" – 2 Peter 1:4 [Emphasis is mine].

You can always know the presence of God because He never leaves you.

".... God has said, "I will never abandon you or leave you" – Hebrews 13:5 GW.

"I have been young, and now am old, yet I have not seen the righteous forsaken, nor his children begging for bread" – Psalm 37:25 NHEB.

You can do all things by Christ Jesus.

"I can do all things through Christ who strengthens me" – Philippians 4:13.

"For it is [not your strength, but it is] God who is effectively at work in you, both to will and to work [that

is, strengthening, energizing, and creating in you the longing and the ability to fulfill your purpose] for His good pleasure" – Philippians 2:13 Amplified Bible.

You have the wisdom of God.

"But it is from Him that you are in Christ Jesus, who became to us wisdom from God [revealing His plan of salvation], and righteousness [making us acceptable to God], and sanctification [making us holy and setting us apart for God], and redemption [providing our ransom from the penalty for sin]" – 1 Corinthians 1:30 Amplified Bible.

"If any of you lacks wisdom [to guide him through a decision or circumstance], he is to ask of [our benevolent] God, who gives to everyone generously and without rebuke or blame, and it will be given to him" – James 1:5 Amplified Bible.

<u>Prayer:</u>

I pray that as you consider and meditate on the above scriptures and many others that reveal your spiritual identity [new nature, new creation] in Christ, may the Lord give you a spirit of wisdom and revelation in the knowledge of Him, so that you may grow into the fulness of His will and fulfill your purpose in Him.

Chapter 3

The Effect of an Undivided Mind

The *mind* is a set of cognitive faculties, which includes our consciousness, perception, thinking, judgement, and memory. It is the capacity of a man's thoughts and consciousness.

The battleground, the soil on which the enemy will try to implant his deceit, his lies, and his subtle suggestions, is none other than the mind. The strongest instrument that the devil will use to fight us is his ability to have access to our mind. When he gains access to our mind, he will control our perception and determine our actions, which will ultimately affect our relationship and walk with the Lord.

Therefore, we must constantly watch over our mind to guard our thoughts, so the enemy will not have access to control us. To do this, we need to renew our minds through the Word of God, as we focus on godly values and ethical attitudes that reflect the character of Christ. This is how we can have victory over the enemy, and not be conformed to the systems of this world.

"And do not be conformed to this world [any longer with its superficial values and customs], but be transformed and progressively changed [as you mature spiritually] by the renewing of your mind [focusing on godly values and ethical attitudes], so that you may prove [for yourselves] what the will of God is, that which is good and acceptable and perfect [in His plan and purpose for you]" – Romans 12:2 Amplified Bible.

"Finally, believers, whatever is true, whatever is honorable and worthy of respect, whatever is right and confirmed by God's word, whatever is pure and wholesome, whatever is lovely and brings peace, whatever is admirable and of good repute; if there is any excellence, if there is anything worthy of praise, think continually on these things [center your mind on them, and implant them in your heart]" – Philippians 4:8 Amplified Bible.

Having considered the renewal of the mind as a key to victory over the world and its lies, we can now turn to the problem of a divided mind. Many times the Scripture warns us of the danger of a divided mind.

"A double minded man is unstable in all his ways" – James 1:8.

"Draw near to God and He will draw near to you Cleanse your hands, you sinners; and purify your hearts, you double-minded" – James 4:8.

James says that a man who doubts God is unstable like the waves of the sea tossed back and forth; he is a double-minded person. <u>Being double-minded results in instability and unanswered prayers</u>. Later in his epistle, James indicates that double-mindedness is sin and that the double-minded man should purify his heart.

Peter also spoke about double-mindedness, but the translators of the Bible called it "cares." The word translated "care(s)" in **1 Peter 5:7** comes from two Greek words. The first word is **'merimna,'** from the root word **'merizo,'** which means **"to part,"** or **"to divide."** The second Greek word is **'nous,'** which means **"the mind."**

Now that we understand this, let us read 1 Peter 5:7 from this perspective - **"Casting all that divides your mind on Him, because He cares for you."**

Many times, especially when we face unbearable circumstances, we struggle between trusting God and looking at our circumstances.

As believers in Christ, we have all been in such situations and faced such challenges. It is amazing how we get distracted, anxious, and worried when things go wrong or do not work out in the way we expected; even when we have prayed, we still doubt. It becomes an issue of double-mindedness and evidence of a lack of trust in the Father who loves us and who makes no mistakes.

It is therefore important to constantly and habitually, as children of God, to renew our mind with the word of God. This will enable us to have stability in our mind and faith in God always.

A person with an undivided mind has focus, and therefore, can effectively accomplish the goal that is set before him or her, and not live in a state of compromise.

Our spiritual mind has the capability of attaining the highest goal, when we feed it with the proper knowledge of God.

Paul tells of the need to focus on those things that can change the direction of our mind, to think on those things that will lead us to freedom in our mind – Philippians 4:8-9.

"For as he thinketh in his heart, so is he...." – Proverbs 23:7a.

This means we are a product of our thoughts, because we become what we think. Therefore, Paul the apostle admonished us not to conform to this world by our thinking, but to transform ourselves by the renewing of our mindset into the image of Christ.

"And be continually renewed in the spirit of your mind [having a fresh, untarnished mental and spiritual attitude], and put on the new self [the regenerated and renewed nature], created in God's image, [God-like] in

the righteousness and holiness of the truth [living in a way that expresses to God your gratitude for your salvation]" – Ephesians 4:23-24 Amplified Bible.

"Don't copy the behavior and customs of this world, but let God transform you into a new person by changing the way you think. Then you will learn to know God's will for you, which is good and pleasing and perfect" - Romans 12:2 NLT.

Like Joseph in Genesis 37, while I was finishing my high school, in the year 2000, the Lord spoke to me about my future. In that dream, the Lord told me he would be taking me out of Nigeria and that I would be going abroad and marrying a foreigner. He also revealed to me that this foreigner would bear my children.

Understanding my background and the family I came from, it seemed impossible for such a dream to be a reality. I came from a family of five children with only a single mother and no income to support us. From the worldly standard, we were poor, even to the poor people.

During this time, our mother instilled something in us. It was the ability to trust in God, even when it did not make sense. Towards the end of 2000, I graduated from high school, and the dream from God kept on ringing in my heart, but I had no idea how it would happen. Like Joseph, a time came when I could not keep my dream to myself. I shared the dream with my mom and my siblings. They were supportive, but I knew deep down inside of them it did not seem realistic. Life continued and I started working for a pharmaceutical company. While I was working there, I was still meditating on and thinking about my future with God.

In 2003, when the pharmaceutical company was no longer working out, my family told me that I needed to go serve a man for seven years. This meant that I would become a slave for seven years with a tiny possibility of being paid wages at the end of my servitude, so that I could start my life. Two years into the agreement, he kicked me out of the house and all hope was lost. All my human efforts had failed, and the only thing left for me was the hope of the promise that God gave to me in 2000. I left his house with nothing, receiving no payment for the work I had done. Then, through the effort of two of my sisters, I was able to set up a business of my own. Three years later, in 2006, again the Lord began to stir up my spirit regarding the dream. I still had no idea of how to make this dream a reality. The need to act on the dream was becoming greater and greater.

In early 2007, I met a former classmate, whom I had not seen in over five years, happened to be traveling, so I called him into my shop and blessed him with a financial offering. As he was leaving my shop, he turned to me and said, "I will not forget this." In April 2007, I received a phone call from him and he said, "I am now in Malaysia and I think there is a great need for men like you here in this land." I began to pray about it and in August, the Lord opened the door for me to travel out of Nigeria to

Malaysia. This would become my first missionary work as an evangelist under Church of God Mission International, led by Pastor Joseph Idika. The first part of my dream was fulfilled.

In 2008, I met my wife, and we got married in 2009. After our wedding, we began to think about and prayerfully consider where we would settle down. On October 29, 2009, I was attending an all-night prayer meeting, when the Lord spoke to me and said, "I am taking you to a nation that you have not been, and from there I will take you to the nations of the world." I said to the Lord, "Now wait a minute, Lord! Have you forgotten that I am from Nigeria, holding a Nigerian passport? How can this be possible?" The Lord said to me, "I will change your identity and when I take you to where you are going, I will establish you. But you must not forget from where I picked you."

I started my process of immigration to Canada, after confirming my mission in Malaysia. I hit a dead end with the Canadian consulate in Malaysia, when they told me that I would **never** enter Canada; their exact words were, "over my dead body." I returned home and my wife and I fasted and prayed for 21 days. At the end of the 21 days, I received an e-mail invitation from the Immigration office, requesting my passport. As I sat in that office, I was faced with the reality that in 48 hours, my Malaysian visa would expire, and I would either be on my way to Canada or heading home to Nigeria. What happened next was nothing short of a miracle. The man who had earlier told me that I would never enter Canada personally handed me my Canadian residence permit. The Bible says, when the ways of a man are pleasing unto God, He makes even his enemies to be at peace with him. In February 2010, I landed in the nation of Canada. God then began to establish my wife and I, just as He had spoken.

As I write this book, I have been to eight nations with a Canadian passport. In February 2018, I will be stepping into my ninth nation. God also blessed my wife and I with five, wonderful children. We continue to further the Kingdom of God, according to His purpose and will for our lives.

In all of this, one thing that kept us going is our undivided focus on the Word of the Lord.

So many of us have become masters at magnifying our problems and minimizing God and His Word, and by doing so, we begin to live in a divided mind condition and a state of compromise.

When we have the right perception of who God is, then we can make God bigger than our problems, and begin to glorify and praise Him for His goodness.

Therefore, it is very important for us as believers to fellowship around likeminded Christians, so that we can learn, and be encouraged by their testimonies and encounters of God's grace and goodness. This will help build our faith in God, and maintain stability in our mind and walk. Our association will always influence our mind and shape who we become.

There is an old saying, "Show me your friends and I'll tell you who you are," because your circle of friends has a great influence in the achievement of your God-giving purpose.

Your association can become a strong influence in your mind and walk with the Lord, which can be dangerous and become a distraction to your kingdom assignment and purpose, if you allow the negativity drive to control you.

An example of a positive influence of association was Jonathan and David in the Bible. They had a wholesome and pure friendship, which was very vital in David's life in becoming a king. Jonathan was a wise counsellor who played a very significant role in the life of David through the process of him becoming the king of Israel. His friendship helped save his life from his father; Saul who would have killed him and aborted his God-given assignment as a king.

"He who walks with wise men will be wise, But the companion of fools will suffer harm" – **Proverbs 13:30.**

For the fulfilment of our divine purpose and destiny, we need true associations who will be wise and positive influences in our thinking, to position us accurately. We need friends that we can be completely open and transparent with, have complete trust in and confide in, so they can bring wise and godly counsel to us.

How to Have a Renewed Mind:

When our mind is renewed, we will know and understand God's will for our lives and have peace within. For us to renew *our minds we* must follow the Holy Spirit's initiatives, which will bring about this transformation.

1. Meditating Daily on God's Word.

To meditate on God's Word is to think deeply and focus one's mind for a period on God's teachings and promises. This can be done in silence, or by proclaiming the Word to ourselves over and over again, until the Word becomes a part of our heart, and we can then walk in obedience to this Word. This is how we can see the manifestation of God's Word in and through us, as our faith is built in Christ.

"Only be strong and very courageous; be careful to do according to all the law which Moses My servant commanded you; do not turn from it to the right or to the left, so that you may have success wherever you go. This book of the law shall not depart from your mouth, but you shall meditate on it day and night, so that you may be careful to do according to all that is written in it; for then you will make your way prosperous, and then you will have success" – Joshua 1:7-8 NASB.

2. Seeking the Lord's guidance in all things:

Everything starts in the mind, so we must always ask the Lord to fill our mind with the knowledge of His will as we acknowledge Him in all our ways, and by so doing we can always have the right perception in all things.

"Trust in and rely confidently on the Lord with all your heart and do not rely on your own insight or understanding. In all your ways know and acknowledge and recognize Him, and He will make your paths straight and smooth [removing obstacles that block your way]. Do not be wise in your own eyes; Fear the Lord [with reverent awe and obedience] and turn [entirely] away from evil" – **Proverbs 3:5-7 Amplified Bible.**

This must always be our prayer and heart's desire as we seek the Lord's guidance and will in all things.

3. Resting in the Truth of the Reality of Your Identity in Christ:

When we are fully grounded in our identity of who we are in Christ, and the reality of our New Creation, we can keep our mind focused on God. It will also bring an assurance of peace with God.

Our identity in Christ is the principal fact that influences and controls our present circumstances and it determines our eternal future. Therefore, we must rest in it without any shadow of doubt. Always remember that God is faithful to His promises to you.

4. Praying Constantly in the Holy Spirit:

Praying in the Spirit has the power to supernaturally transform our mind and change things around us. This act releases the Holy Spirit to take charge of things, and bring into reality the mind and will of God for us.

"So too the [Holy] Spirit comes to our aid and bears us up in our weakness; for we do not know what prayer to offer nor how to offer it worthily as we ought, but the Spirit Himself goes to meet our supplication and pleads in our behalf with unspeakable yearnings and groanings too deep for utterance. And He Who searches the hearts of men knows what is in the mind of the [Holy] Spirit [what His intent is], because the Spirit intercedes and pleads [before God] in behalf of the saints according to and in harmony with God's will" – Romans 8:26-27 Amplified Bible.

"And be renewed in the spirit of your mind" – Ephesians 4:23.

When we constantly pray in the Spirit, our mind is renewed according to the will of God.

5. Changing Self-Focused Thoughts to God-focused Thinking:

The essence of the Adamic nature [the mind of the flesh] is the shift from a *God-centeredness* to a *self-centeredness*, and this affects our perception of God and His viewpoint. This means that we must *replace self-focused thinking* with a *God-focused mindset*. This can only be done when we follow the leading of the Holy Spirit in all things and allow Him to guide us in our walk. By so doing we can always examine our thoughts with the Word [God's will] and change our thinking, as we focus on God's will.

"Now the mind of the flesh [which is sense and reason without the Holy Spirit] is death [death that comprises all the miseries arising from sin, both here and hereafter]. But the mind of the [Holy] Spirit is life and [soul] peace [both now and forever]. [That is] because the mind of the flesh [with its carnal thoughts and purposes] is hostile to God, for it does not submit itself to God's Law; indeed it cannot. So then those who are living the life of the flesh [catering to the appetites and impulses of their carnal nature] cannot please or satisfy God, or be acceptable to Him. But you are not living the life of the flesh, you are living the life of the Spirit, if the [Holy] Spirit of God [really] dwells within you [directs and controls you]. But if anyone does not possess the [Holy] Spirit of Christ, he is none of His [he does not belong to Christ, is not truly a child of God]. But if Christ lives in you, [then although] your [natural] body is dead by reason of sin and guilt, the spirit is alive because of [the]

righteousness [that He imputes to you]. And if the Spirit of Him Who raised up Jesus from the dead dwells in you, [then] He Who raised up Christ Jesus from the dead will also restore to life your mortal (short-lived, perishable) bodies through His Spirit Who dwells in you" – **Romans 8: 6-11 Amplified Bible.**

When we have a mind that is dedicated and pure to God, we will desire to do the things that will glorify our Father. A mind that is renewed with the Word of God will always seek to glorify God.

When your mind is wrapped up with the imagination of the goodness of God, the devil will not have any room to work on you.

Imagination is much more important than people realize. The Word of God comes alive when one can picture what the Lord is saying. When God's Word controls our imagination [as we meditate - read and think about the word], we will begin to see the manifestation of things in the Scriptures that we cannot see with our physical eyes.

When we use our imagination to see and perceive ourselves in the way God sees us, we will become what we imagine.

Our mind controls what we say and what we do. When we try to change our actions without renewing our mind, the results will never be permanent. If people want their behavior to change, they must ultimately focus on renewing their mind.

The Scripture makes it abundantly clear that the condition of our mind is far more important than our actions. I pray we do not limit God with our mind, because a renewed mind is the key to accurate thinking and kingdom perception as we allow the Holy Spirit to work through us.

It is a very dangerous thing to live in a divided mind. A divided mind is the devil's workshop. Genesis 11:1-7 tells us about what an undivided mind can accomplish. Even God recognizes and affirms an undivided mind.

KINGDOM PERCEPTION

Developing Accurate Understanding Of Kingdom Principles

Chapter 4

Accessing His Presence

"According to His eternal purpose that He accomplished in Christ Jesus our Lord. In Him and through faith in Him we may approach God with freedom and confidence" - Ephesians 3:11-12 NIV.

There is a great need for us to have the right perception of God and our relationship with Him, because it will ultimately determine our attitude and approach to Him. God's eternal plan, which He carried out through Christ Jesus, our Lord, is for us to have unrestricted access to His presence as His sons.

Now that we are saved, we must know and understand that we are the sons of God and citizens of heaven. This means that we should approach God with the mindset that He is our Father.

"But to as many as did receive and welcome Him, He gave the right [the authority, the privilege] to become children of God, that is, to those who believe in (adhere to, trust in, and rely on) His name" - John 1:12 Amplified Bible.

"He has delivered us from the domain of darkness and transferred us to the kingdom of His beloved Son" - Colossians 1:13 ESV.

"But we are citizens of heaven and are eagerly waiting for our Savior to come from there. Our Lord Jesus Christ" - Philippians 3:20 CEV.

In addition to our knowledge of His deity as God and our acceptance of Him as a Saviour, there is a need for us to know Him as our Father.

In what is popularly known as "The Lord's Prayer" in Matthew 6:9, Jesus taught His disciples how to pray, saying, *"This is how you should pray: Our Father in heaven...."* - Matthew 6:9.

"Pray, then, [in this way: 'Our Father, who is in heaven, Hallowed be Your name'. 'Your kingdom come, Your will be done on earth as it is in heaven'. 'Give us this day our [daily bread'. 'And forgive us our debts, as we have forgiven our debtors [letting go of both the wrong and the resentment]'. 'And do not lead us into temptation, but deliver us from evil'. [For Yours is the kingdom and the power and the glory forever. Amen.]"
– Matthew 6:9-13 Amplified Bible.

'**Our Father:**' This affirms personal relationship with God as Your Father. We need to understand that Jesus has directed us to pray, not to our Lord, not to God, but to **OUR FATHER.** This is intimate; this is a relationship and it affirms who we are within the Kingdom. The understanding of this will ultimately change the way we approach God, our Father.

'In heaven, Hallowed be Your name:' Recognizes Him as Lord of all, honoring Him as living, powerful and real.

'Your kingdom come:' Accept God's right to directly rule your life. There is a need for us to yield ourselves, along with our desires, to the will of God.

'Your will be done on earth, as it is in heaven:' This is a complete submission of our lives to God's will, which is already done in heaven, so we become a reflection of His will here on earth, as it is in heaven. By this, we become the instrument for the fulfilment of God's will and purpose here on earth.

'Give us this day our daily bread:' Recognizing God's involvement in your daily experiences, in the supply of all your needs. By this, we acknowledge Him as our source – Our Jehovah Jireh.

'And forgive us our debts, as we have forgiven our debtors:' This is an expression of readiness to live as a forgiving and forgiven person **[letting go of both the wrong and the resentments, just as God has forgiven us of all our wrong doings]**.

'**And do not lead us into temptation, but deliver us from evil.'** Asking for protection from the trials and temptations the evil one will bring to us, that will become a distraction and hindrance to our walk with Christ, and for the advancement of God's Kingdom here on earth, through us.

'**For Yours is the Kingdom, and the Power and the Glory forever.'** When God's Kingdom (His will and His reign) is established in us, His Power and His Glory will be manifested in and through us. This is the Father's desire for us as we seek Him in our prayer and develop our relationship with Him as Father and son.

We must understand that God our Father is not mad at us, because God is a Person and can have a relationship with us. His intent for us has always been for us to have a relationship with Him.

For many of us, the word "father" is a negative word that brings back bad memories, because of our experiences, and we think that if God is like our earthly father, then we do not want anything to do with God.

The truth is that earthly fathers can make their homes hell-fire on earth. Human fathers can choose when they want to love you and when they do not. They can be moody, abusive, controlling, alcoholic and even violent. Because of this, when the word "Father" is mentioned, it carries many negative connotations for some of us.

One of the reasons many people are not able to connect with God is because they subconsciously think that God is like their earthly father, who may have been unaccommodating, so they think God is unaccommodating. Maybe their father was undependable or untrustworthy, so they think that God is undependable and untrustworthy too. They impose all of those messed up thoughts, hurts and emotions about God being a Father, and it is no wonder that they have a hard time connecting with Him.

Many kids in this 21st century have little or no connection to their earthly father. So why would they be expected to have a connection with their heavenly Father?

We must let go of the wrong perception and misconceptions that we have about God the Father, so that we can begin to understand the truth of who God the Father is and what He is like.

When we know the truth of Who our Father God is, the truth will set us free! Wrong perception will always keep us disconnected from God. However, when we understand and have the right perception of Him (God, as our Father), we are going to love Him as we have never done before.

It is, therefore, imperative for us to understand that God is a multifaceted God. Just like a diamond with a multifaceted surface. If you look at it from different angles, it reflects the underlying symmetry of the crystal structure, light and beauty. This is the same with God. He has different aspects of His divine nature and attributes beyond human comprehension. For example, the revelation of His names in different epoch reveals His nature.

"Then God spoke further to Moses and said to him, "I am the Lord. I appeared to Abraham, to Isaac, and to Jacob (Israel) as God Almighty [El Shaddai], but by My name, Lord [Yahweh], I did not make Myself known to them [in acts and great miracles]" - Exodus 6:2-3 **Amplified Bible.**

We must shift our perception beyond the position of constantly seeing ourselves as sinners, always in need of a Saviour, to an accurate position and understanding that we are sons, and this is the way the Lord wants us to relate to Him - as our Father.

In Christ Jesus, we are no longer a sinner. We are now saints [and sons of God]. Our old Adamic nature of sin has been done away with in Christ. Our faith and acceptance of Jesus has given us the entitlement of sonship.

"So then, from now on we do not think of anyone from a human point of view. Even if we did think of the Messiah (Christ) from a human point of view, we don't think of Him that way anymore. Therefore, if anyone is in the Messiah, he is a new creation. Old things have

disappeared, and - look! - all things have become new!" -
2 Corinthians 5:16-17 ISV.

We are a new creation in Christ and this gives us access to His presence.

We must not allow religion or the philosophy of men to mislead us to believe that we are still sinners, always in need of a Saviour. This will rob us of our authority as a new creation, and the privilege of sonship, which we received in Christ Jesus, through our faith and trust in His name.

One of the lies of Satan that he uses to trick believers is to remind them of their past mistakes to create a consciousness of sin, guilt and judgement. By so doing, they now see themselves as sinners [instead of sons], which now affect their perception, and ultimately, their position in Christ and their approach to God. Therefore, many believers are under a guilty verdict when they come before the Lord in prayer and they spend most of their time confessing their past sins which has already been done away with through the sacrifice of Christ.

In Christ Jesus, we are no longer under a guilty verdict, because there is now no condemnation to them who are in Christ Jesus.

"Therefore, there is now no condemnation [no guilty verdict, no punishment] for those who are in Christ Jesus

[who believe in Him as personal Lord and Savior]" -
Romans 8:1 Amplified Bible.

We are free from the standards of sin and guilt. Let us therefore approach God as our Father, because we are His sons.

In speaking about the pattern and principle of the Kingdom of God, Jesus often revealed deep truths by using children as an illustration of how our lifestyle should be as members of His Kingdom.

"I assure you and most solemnly say to you, unless you repent [that is, change your inner self—your old way of thinking, live changed lives] and become like children [trusting, humble, and forgiving], you will never enter the kingdom of heaven" - Matthew 18:3 Amplified.

We must change our perception [our old way of thinking], and become like children.

As a father of five children, I give my children unrestricted access to me anytime, as they know they are sons and daughters, and not strangers and foreigners in the house. They know their positions as sons in the house and this understanding, which is deeply rooted in them, allows them to always come to me without fear, guilt conscience or condemnation, because they are confident of their father's love [despite their childish mistakes and past issues].

The sacrifice of Jesus Christ has already dealt with our sinful nature once and for all.

"By God's will we have been sanctified once and for all through the sacrifice of the body of Jesus, the Messiah (Jesus Christ)" - Hebrews 10:10 ISV.

The heart of the Father is a heart of love. God's love is unchanging, despite our condition and the state of our lives [even though He is not pleased with our actions, He still loves us and does not impute our unrighteousness against us]. By this love, we can confidently approach Him, and receive His mercy and grace that He has lavishly poured out upon us.

"Brothers and sisters, because of the blood of Jesus we can now confidently go into the holy place. Jesus has opened a new and living way for us to go through the curtain. (The curtain is his own body.) We have a superior priest in charge of God's house. We have been sprinkled with his blood to free us from a guilty conscience, and our bodies have been washed with clean water. So we must continue to come to him with a sincere heart and strong faith" - Hebrews 10:19-22 GW.

The Parable of the Prodigal Son (also known as the Lost Son, and a Loving Father) is one of the parables of Jesus that appeared in Luke 15:11–32. The story is a good example that reveals the father's heart of love for his son. His son became rebellious, walked away from home with the inheritance, and wasted his fortune in reckless and immoral living. He finally came to his senses and said he would return to his father and say to him he has sinned against heaven and before his sight, and was no longer worthy to be called his son, and for him to be treated as a hired servant.

"And He said, "There was a man who had two sons. And the younger of them said to his father, 'Father, give me the share of property that is coming to me.' And he divided his property between them. Not many days later, the younger son gathered all he had and took a journey into a far country, and there he squandered his property in reckless living. And when he had spent everything, a severe famine arose in that country, and he began to be in need. So he went and hired himself out to one of the citizens of that country, who sent him into his fields to feed pigs. And he was longing to be fed with the pods that the pigs ate, and no one gave him anything. "But when he came to himself, he said, 'How many of my father's hired servants have more than enough bread, but I perish here with hunger! I will arise and go to my father, and I will say to him, "Father, I have sinned against heaven and before you. I am no longer worthy to be called your son. Treat me as one of your hired servants." ' And he arose and came to his father. But while he was still a long way off, his father saw him and felt compassion, and ran and embraced him and kissed him. And the son said to him, 'Father, I have sinned against heaven and before you. I am no longer worthy to be called your son.' But the father said to his servants, 'Bring quickly the best robe, and put it on him, and put

a ring on his hand, and shoes on his feet. And bring the fattened calf and kill it, and let us eat and celebrate. For this my son was dead, and is alive again; he was lost, and is found.' And they began to celebrate" - Luke 15:11-24 ESV.

Notice this: *while he was still a long way off, his father saw him and was moved with compassion (love) for him, and ran and embraced him and kissed him.*

In the mind of the son, he was approaching the father with a slave mentality and a guilty conscience because of his actions, but the father did not see and accept him in that mindset and condition of his action. Instead, the father demonstrated his love for him and received him as his son, welcoming him as a guest of honor with a feast of celebration.

Before he even had the chance to ask the father to receive and treat him as a slave, the father reached out and showed love and acceptance to him. His position was fully restored, and he was given a robe, ring and sandals for his feet.

The robe symbolizes righteousness, honour, beauty, glory and his acceptance and justification shows he is no longer guilty before the Lord.

".... I will forget about their sins and no longer remember their evil deeds"- Hebrews 10:17 CEV.

The ring symbolizes the restoration of his union and the authority he has as a child with his father.

The sandal symbolizes a new walk of freedom from the past [the mindset of guilt and slavery], to the restoration of his sonship in the house (or kingdom).

The father's love was so overwhelming, but the son's perception made him feel undeserving. Yet, the father's love brought acceptance, healing and restoration of a renewed purpose of his position.

When we have the right perception of who God is to us as a Father [and we as His sons], then we will be able to embrace His love towards us. God's love is broad, and it covers every spectrum of our lives and relationship with Him.

Jesus Christ, Who is the 'Pattern Son,' clearly illustrates this for us in His prayers to God, as He addresses Him as Father.

"These words spake Jesus, and lifted up his eyes to heaven, and said, Father, the hour is come; glorify thy Son, that thy Son also may glorify thee:" - John 17:1.

"For this reason [grasping the greatness of this plan by which Jews and Gentiles are joined together in Christ] I bow my knees [in reverence] before the Father [of our Lord Jesus Christ], from whom every family in heaven

and on earth derives its name [God—the first and ultimate Father]". - Ephesians 3:14-15 Amplified Bible.

Christ's sacrificial blood opens the way for us, not only to be reconciled to God, our Lord and Creator, but to also embrace our loving and eternal God as our Father.

The good news is that regardless of how well or poorly our earthly father treated us, God's Fatherhood is eternal, and our ability to grasp this concept will ultimately affect our relationship and approach to God as our Father.

We must not lose the essence of His Fatherhood because this is what defines our relationship with Him, and gives us access, by faith in Christ Jesus and through His Spirit, into His presence.

"Whom we have boldness and confident access through faith in Him [that is, our faith gives us sufficient courage to freely and openly approach God through Christ]" - Ephesians 3:12 Amplified Bible.

KINGDOM PERCEPTION

Developing Accurate Understanding Of Kingdom Principles

Chapter 5

Increasing Your Desire To Know God

"But more than that, <u>I count everything as loss compared to the priceless privilege and supreme advantage of knowing Christ Jesus my Lord [and of growing more deeply and thoroughly acquainted with Him—a joy unequaled]</u>. For His sake I have lost everything, and I consider it all garbage, so that I may gain Christ, and may be found in Him [believing and relying on Him], not having any righteousness of my own derived from [my obedience to] the Law and its rituals, but [possessing] that [genuine righteousness] which comes through faith in Christ, the righteousness which comes from God on the basis of faith. And this, <u>so that I may know Him [experientially, becoming more thoroughly acquainted with Him, understanding the remarkable wonders of His Person more completely]</u> and [in that same way experience] the power of His resurrection [which overflows and is active in believers], and [that I may share] the fellowship of His sufferings, by being continually conformed [inwardly into His likeness even] to His death [dying as He did]" – Philippians 3:8-10 Amplified Bible.

Life's greatest privilege, as a believer in Christ Jesus, is to know God. It is a priceless privilege to grow more deeply, and to become acquainted with Him. This can only be achieved when there is a strong desire in our heart for God and a willingness to obey Him.

The reason why so many believers are walking in ignorance is that there is no desperate desire in their heart for God. So many have lost their passion and desire to know God, hence we are not seeing the mighty power of God at work within and among us.

"Do you not believe that I am in the Father, and the Father is in Me? The words I say to you I do not say on My own initiative or authority, but the Father, abiding continually in Me, does His works [His attesting miracles and acts of power]. Believe Me that I am in the Father and the Father is in Me; otherwise believe [Me] because of the [very] works themselves [which you have witnessed]. I assure you and most solemnly say to you, anyone who believes in Me [as Savior] will also do the things that I do; and he will do even greater things than these [in extent and outreach], because I am going to the Father - John 14:10-12 Amplified Bible.

Throughout the Scriptures, we read of great men and women who were used by the power of God to do great and mighty things for the Lord. These men and women were ordinary people like us, but they developed a strong desire to know God and to experience Him and His power.

"<u>Elijah was a man with a nature like ours [with the same physical, mental, and spiritual limitations and shortcomings], and he prayed intensely</u> for it not to rain, and it did not rain on the earth for three years and six months" – James 5:17.

The intensity of Elijah's prayer was birthed out of His desire for God, just like Paul, who was so desperate in His desire to know God. I believe we are yet to conceive and comprehend the tremendous power that there is in a desire. In order to see the power of God move in a supernatural way in this 21st century, we must become a people who are desperately desire to know God, and to be known by God.

A desire will establish a strong foundation through which we can know God, build a mountain moving faith and a powerful prayer life.

You may be asking, what do you mean by this? What is desire?

A desire is defined as a strong feeling or wish for something. Oftentimes, we use the word incorrectly, and we do not have an intense passion and motivation to do anything in our walk and pursuit to know God. Most believers are just wishing, hoping and wanting to know God, but there is no burning or deep yearning to know God.

King David was a man just like us, but he had a heart for God. His heart's desire was not just a mere wish for God, but it was a deep longing and thirst in his heart for the presence of God that motivated him. He was very passionate about his desire for God.

"As the deer pants [longingly] for the water brooks, So my soul pants [longingly] for You, O God. My soul thirsts for God, for the living God. When will I come and see the face of God?" – Psalm 42:1-2.

"My soul (my life, my inner self) longs for and greatly desires the courts of the Lord...." – Psalm 84:2a **Amplified Bible.**

Like King David, we must have a strong passion for God - an unsatisfied, holy appetite that springs from a deep desire to know God *more than we know Him.*

Moses is another man who had a strong desire for God. When he encountered God at the burning bush and received his divine commission to lead the children of Israel out of Egypt into the Promised Land, his desire became very strong, because he now knew God in a unique way. God had revealed and proven Himself to him. This led him to accomplish what God had called him to do.

A strong, deep desire is a concept that makes our lives and shapes our destiny. It is a passion, which comes out of a right perception of knowing who God is.

Very few people are attaining to a higher level of success because of their understanding of this passionate desire burning within their soul. As we increase continually in the knowledge of God's Word, it will create within us an intense desire to know more of God and to fulfill His Word.

Paul J. Meyer said, "*A burning desire is the greatest motivator of any human action. The desire for success implants success consciousness, which in turn creates a vigorous and ever-increasing habit of success.*"

"*He told them, "I have eagerly desired to eat this Passover meal with you before I suffer"* – Luke 22:15.

In this chapter of the Scripture, Jesus uses the word 'desire,' because He is showing His disciples His intent, and how important it is for Him to have this meal (last supper) with them before His departure. The purpose of His desire was to have fellowship and communion with His disciples. Likewise, we must also desire and crave to have fellowship and communion with God, as this will bring us into a deeper knowledge of Him. The secret key of knowing Him is the desire to know Him.

A right perception of God will increase our desire to know God. Having a right perception leads us to deepen our knowledge and vision about God.

Knowledge will set a flame within us. It is like a machine, but vision produces the strong desire - the power that now drives the machinery.

A deep desire is produced when we combine 'knowledge' and 'vision.'

When we walk with the knowledge of God and a clear vision [a prophetic perception of God], it will produce a deep desire in us that will drive us to know Him more.

Knowledge:

"My people are destroyed for lack of knowledge: because thou hast rejected knowledge, I will also reject thee...." - Hosea 4:6.

Vision:

"Where there is no vision, the people perish......." - Proverbs 29:18.

A vision is a prophetic revelation (light) of God's eternal purpose that we receive for the fulfilment of our life and ministry.

Now these two verses teach us two things:

1. People *without knowledge* are in danger of destruction.
2. People *without vision* are perishing.

Real Desire produces Real Faith.

It is true that faith comes through our hearing and knowledge of the word (Romans 10:17). However, knowledge on its own is not enough. The application of knowledge produces faith and results.

If you know that a medication can relieve you of your pain and you refuse to take it, the pain will not go away.

The knowledge of the Word of God, which we have inside of us, will bring us into a dimension of the revelation and realities of God when we act upon it.

"This book of the law shall not depart out of thy mouth; but thou shalt meditate therein day and night, that thou mayest observe to do according to all that is written therein: <u>for then thou shalt make thy way prosperous, and then thou shalt have good success</u>" – Joshua 1:8.

"Now it shall be, if you diligently listen to and obey the voice of the Lord your God, being careful to do all of His commandments which I am commanding you today, the Lord your God will set you high above all the nations of the earth"- Deuteronomy 28:1.

Many people know God's promises but never act upon it because they lack that deep and intense desire. Deep and strong desire will cause us to not only know God's promises for our lives, but also to consistently think on them, speak them, rejoice in them, and act on them - this is how real faith is produced. It is this kind of faith, born out of a strong desire, which produces vision.

How To Increase Your Desire For God

Our desire for God can be increased by <u>our love for Him,</u> through our <u>constant communication with Him.</u>

Communication is a very vast instrument in a relationship. When I first met my wife in 2008, we talked on the phone for hours, discussing our future, how many children we would love to have, the type of house we were going to buy and live in, and many other things. What was so wonderful about this was that the more we talked, the more we knew and understood things about ourselves, and the more our desire and love for each other grew stronger. The passion to live with each other became irresistible.

After our wedding, we lived apart from each other for eight months. She was living in Canada, while I was living in the nation of Malaysia. There were many occasions, when I was at work in Malaysia, all I could think about was going back home to make a phone call, just to hear her voice. Through our constant communications, we were able to keep the fire of our love and marriage alive until I finally moved to Canada to live with her permanently.

It is the will of God that His children would come to Him and communicate with Him daily.

"Come to Me, all who are weary and heavily burdened [by religious rituals that provide no peace], and

I will give you rest [refreshing your souls with salvation]. Take My yoke upon you and learn from Me [following Me as My disciple], for I am gentle and humble in heart, and you will find rest (renewal, blessed quiet) for your souls. For My yoke is easy [to bear] and My burden is light." - Mathew 11:28-30 Amplified Bible.

"Call to Me and I will answer you, and tell you [and even show you] great and mighty things, [things which have been confined and hidden], which you do not know and understand and cannot distinguish". - Jeramiah 33:3 Amplified Bible.

When we understand the heart of God for us and His will and purpose, our desire to know Him will increase.

"O taste and see that the Lord [our God] is good; How blessed [fortunate, prosperous, and favored by God] is the man who takes refuge in Him" – Psalm 34:8 Amplified Bible.

When we go to God through prayer and trust Him with all of our needs, we will understand that the more we encounter His presence, the more we will hunger and desire for Him.

The most wonderful thing about it is that **we will discover that no matter how much we long for God, and how much we want Him, His desire for us is greater. Therefore, when our delight is in the Lord, He will give us the desires of our heart.**

"Delight yourself in the Lord and He will give you the desires of your heart" – Psalm 37:4.

"Ask and keep on asking and it will be given to you; seek and keep on seeking and you will find; knock and keep on knocking and the door will be opened to you" - Mathew 7:7 Amplified Bible.

Psalm 20:4 says, *"May He give you the desires of your heart and make all your plans succeed"*

Communication requires discipline, dedication and commitment so we can increase our desire for God and develop a healthy relationship with Him.

Doing nothing results in nothing. If we are going to see a significant increase in our desire for God, we must discipline ourselves and remove anything that will constitute a hindrance to our time with the Father. This may involve shutting off our phones, TV, and any form of distraction, to have undivided time with our Father.

"But Jesus Himself would often slip away to the wilderness and pray" - Luke 5:16 New American Standard Version.

Jesus is a clear example of one with a dedicated relationship with the Father. It was His habit to constantly retire to a deserted place to pray [as He spent time in communication with His Father]. The Scripture shows that Jesus often withdrew from the multitude to communicate with His Father. This speaks of His dedication and commitment to His relationship with the Father.

I was at a men's conference earlier this year when the speaker asked the men to form groups and talk about what they think might be the reason they don't spend time with God. I was very surprised and amazed by the answers from some of the men. Some said they were very busy and had no time to pray or meditate on the Word of God, and others said they didn't have a private place, etc. I said to one of the men, 'I want to ask you a question,' and he said, 'go ahead.' I asked him what his favorite game was, and he said, 'baseball.' I said, 'good.' I then asked him when the last time he had watched a baseball game was. He said he had just watched a game the night before. Then I asked him, 'for how many hours?' He said, 'for about two hours.' I said, 'that is great. How did you get the time to watch the game?' No comment! Then I said to him, 'your problem is not time, but lack of a passionate desire for God.' I said to him, 'for as long as you live, you will never have time because you cannot buy time, but we make and dedicate time for things that are important to us.'

One thing that was very clear about those men was the lack of desire, passion and dedication to be alone with the Lord.

Let's consider these quotes:

"One of the best gifts we can give ourselves is time alone with God" – Joyce Meyer.

"It has been said that no great work in literature or in science was ever wrought by a man who did not love solitude. We may lay it down as an elemental principle of religion, that no large growth in holiness was ever gained by one who did not take time to be often long alone with God" – Austin Phelps.

"If God doesn't want something for me, I shouldn't want it either. Spending time in meditative prayer, getting to know God, helps align my desires with God's" - Phillips Brooks.

"If a man wants to be used by God, he cannot spend all of his time with people." – A. W. Tozer.

"Come now, and let us reason together," Says the Lord. "Though your sins are like scarlet, they shall be as white as snow; Though they are red like crimson, they shall be like wool" - Isaiah 1:18 Amplified Bible.

Nowhere can we get to know the holiness of God, and come under His influence and power, except in the inner chamber. It has been well said: "No man can expect to make progress in holiness who is not often and long alone with God." - Andy Murray.

Chapter 6

Accurate Perception for Effective Leadership

The principles by which the Kingdom of God functions are exactly opposite to the common thinking of man and the generally accepted structure of earthly kingdoms. Therefore, if our life and actions as a leader [whether in a local church or in a secular world] is still in conformity with the pattern of the world, something is wrong. It means that we don't have the right perception of the Kingdom, and our actions will be void of the intent and purpose of God for His Kingdom.

Our perception reveals the way we interpret our experience. OUR PERCEPTION WILL ALWAYS AFFECT OR DETERMINE HOW WE LEAD.

Therefore, having the right perception is a very significant skill for effective leadership. If we are going to lead the people of God to fulfill their God-given purpose in life and ministry, it is paramount that we have the right perception of the Kingdom of God and how it functions, which will ultimately influence our leadership.

Many people have assumed the position of a leader just for what they can attain from it or because of the portfolio that comes with it. However, leadership in the Kingdom of God has never been about what we can get; rather it is a service to the King and His Kingdom. Therefore, having the right perception of God's original intent and purpose for leadership is a doorway to effective service in the Kingdom of God.

When you study the lives of the most influential Christian leaders of our time, such as the late Archbishop Benson Idahosa, Martin Luther King, Jr., and Dr. Myles Munroe among others, you will agree with me that there is one thing they all have in common - the heart to SERVE.

There is no question that the most admired, respected and honored Christian leader of all ages was our Lord Jesus Christ. It is imperative that we study His leadership style, as this will ultimately help us have the right perception of His leadership, as it was clearly demonstrated to us in the Scriptures.

"... just as the Son of Man did not come to be served, but to serve and to give His life as a ransom for many." - Matthew 20:28 Amplified Bible.

Jesus taught, led and trained His people. How did He do this? He did it by serving. Jesus came to serve, and He showed us how to serve through His lifestyle with those in His 'inner circle,' His twelve disciples. As the time of His death approached, He prepared Himself for the cross in the upper room at the last supper, surrounded by those He loved. John 13:1 says, *"Having loved His own who were in the world, He now showed them the full extent of His love."* He then instructed them on His intent for leadership.

"...that Jesus, knowing that the Father had put everything into His hands, and that He had come from God and was [now] returning to God, <u>⁴got up from supper, took off His [outer] robe, and taking a [servant's] towel, He tied it around His waist. Then He poured water into the basin and began washing the disciples' feet and wiping them with the towel which was tied around His waist.</u> When He came to Simon Peter, he said to Him, "Lord, are You going to wash my feet?" Jesus replied to him, "You do not realize now what I am doing, but you will [fully] understand it later." Peter said to Him, "You will never wash my feet!" Jesus answered, "Unless I wash you, you have no part with Me [we can have nothing to do with each other]." Simon Peter said to Him, "Lord, [in that case, wash] not only my feet, but also my hands and my head!" Jesus said to him, "Anyone who has bathed needs only to wash his feet, and is completely clean. And you [My disciples] are clean, but not all of you." For He knew who was going to betray Him; for that reason He said, "Not all of you are clean." <u>So when He had washed their feet and put on His [outer] robe and reclined at the table again, He said to them, "Do you understand what I have done for you? You call Me Teacher and Lord, and you are right in doing so, for that is who I am. So if I, the Lord and the Teacher, washed your feet, you ought to wash one another's feet as well. For I gave you [this as] an example,</u>

<u>*so that you should do [in turn] as I did to you.*</u> - John 13:1-17.

"But Jesus called them to Himself and said, "You know that the rulers of the Gentiles have absolute power and lord it over them, and their great men exercise authority over them [tyrannizing them]. It is not this way among you, but whoever wishes to become great among you shall be your servant, and whoever wishes to be first among you shall be your [willing and humble] slave; just as the Son of Man did not come to be served, but to serve, and to give His life as a ransom for many [paying the price to set them free from the penalty of sin]." - Matt 20:25-28.

"But it is not to be this way with you; on the contrary, the one who is the greatest among you must become like the youngest [and least privileged], and the [one who is the] leader, like the servant" - Luke 22:26.

"But this is not how it is among you; instead, whoever wishes to become great among you must be your servant, and whoever wishes to be first and most important among you must be slave of all" - Mark 10:43-44.

In the preceding Scriptures, we see Jesus not only addressing the issue of leadership and how it is done by the worldly standards, but also establishing a standard of leadership on how the Kingdom of God functions.

"It shall not be so among you...." – **Luke 22:26a.** Clearly, Jesus said we must not model the standard of the world in our service of leadership to be lord over the people, but to demonstrate true humility and servanthood.

Although worldly standards and earthly kingdoms accept certain principles in their leadership style, we must not copy them. The world's standards would tell us that it is the "survival of the fittest."

Worldly leadership is built upon personal gain and desire to move ahead at any cost. However, when we have the right perception of the Kingdom of God, our principles and patterns must be different from that of the world. <u>Our leadership must reflect the teachings of Jesus, and more than that, the example of His own leadership as a servant leader</u>.

For the spiritual leaders of today to accurately and effectively lead the Church of Jesus Christ, our correct perception of Kingdom living is necessary for understanding spiritual teachings, and in giving the right interpretation and revelation in dealing with the people of God.

Having the right perception will affect our attitude and our actions, which will ultimately determine the results we will receive from God.

Throughout the Scriptures, Jesus has clearly shown us the pattern and principle of His leadership, which He Himself instituted, as King over His Kingdom. We must follow His order as subjects of His kingdom to demonstrate this same principle and pattern.

Lead with Love:

One of the keys to effective leadership is to **lead with love.** It is impossible to lead just by commanding people without being compassionate. An effective leader will know and care about what inspires and empowers the people they are leading. It is about caring enough to know what is important to them; caring enough to come down to their level to see them with the eye of Christ, which is the eye of Love, and helping them succeed. Furthermore, an effective leader in the Kingdom will understand the needs of those being led, their weaknesses, and what is required to motivate them to move them forward in fulfilling their God-given destiny. Leading with love is one of the most important tools in becoming a successful leader. To lead effectively, you must love the people you are leading.

As a Kingdom citizen, we must learn to deal with people according to the pattern and principle laid out by the Lord Jesus Christ Himself. He said, **"Love your neighbor as I have loved you."**

When this sacrificial mindset becomes the standard through which we view our fellow human, it is then that we can begin to love and care for them, as our Lord Jesus Christ did.

"And you shall love the Lord your God with all your heart, and with all your soul (life), and with all your mind (thought, understanding), and with all your strength.' This is the second: 'You shall [unselfishly] love your neighbor as yourself.' There is no other commandment greater than these." - Mark 12:30-31 Amplified Bible.

"By this everyone will know that you are My disciples, if you have love and unselfish concern for one another." - John 13:35 Amplified Bible.

Jesus made it very clear that love must be the yardstick for measurement. A true leader reveals his heart by how he loves the people he is leading. We also see love in action in the life of the apostle Paul.

"<u>Therefore [on the basis of these facts], though I have enough confidence in Christ to order you to do what is appropriate, yet for love's sake I prefer to appeal to you—since I am such a person as Paul, an old man, and now also a prisoner [for the sake] of Christ Jesus.</u> I appeal to you for my [own spiritual] child Onesimus, whom I have fathered [in the faith] while a captive in these chains. Once he was useless to you, but now he is indeed useful to you as well as to me. I have sent him back to you in person, that is, like sending my very heart. I would have chosen to keep him with me, so that he might minister to me on your behalf during my imprisonment for the gospel; but I did not want to do anything without first getting your consent, so that your

goodness would not be, in effect, by compulsion but of your own free will. Perhaps it was for this reason that he was separated from you for a while, so that you would have him back forever, <u>no longer as a slave, but [as someone] more than a slave, as a brother [in Christ], especially dear to me, but how much more to you, both in the flesh [as a servant] and in the Lord [as a fellow believer]</u>" – Philemon 1: 8-16 Amplified Bible.

As Paul was in prison in Rome, he became the spiritual mentor and close friend of a runaway slave named Onesimus, whose owner was Philemon. When Paul wrote to Philemon, a leader of the church in Colossae, asking him to receive Onesimus as a brother in Christ, he showed love and diplomacy in the way he talked to Philemon. He said, **'Although in Christ I could be bold and order you to do what you ought to do, yet I prefer to appeal to you on the basis of love. . . . [Onesimus] is very dear to me but even dearer to you, both as a fellow man and as a brother in the Lord'**

The call of leadership within the kingdom of God, whether as a pastor, a worship leader, an usher, small group leader, or any other position of leadership, is a great privilege and a crucial call that spiritual leaders of today must honor and respect. We must understand that being called to lead in Kingdom work at any level is a magnificent act of grace. We see Paul the apostle talking to the elders in Ephesus, telling them that Jesus purchased the church with His own blood and that the Holy Spirit appointed them as an overseer in His church. Therefore, they must love and care for them (the church).

"Take care and be on guard for yourselves and for the whole flock over which the Holy Spirit has appointed you as overseers, to shepherd (tend, feed, guide) the church of God which He bought with His own blood" - Act 20:28 Amplified Bible.

Lead with Humility:

I have been privileged to minister the Word of God in the nations that God has sent me to. During that time, I have had the opportunity to meet many church leaders, wonderful men and women of God. On the other hand, I have also met others who have great anointing, however, their own selfish motives are very transparent, and it was clear that they were working to fulfill their own agenda, rather than the agenda of God. In their attempt to fulfill their own needs, they have taken advantage of the people through their leadership position. The position that they are holding has become a tool in their hands to accomplish their personal gain.

As I begin to study the writings of the apostle Peter to the leaders of the church, I see Peter correcting the errors found in the church leadership:

"Therefore, I strongly urge the elders among you [pastors, spiritual leaders of the church], as a fellow elder and as an eyewitness [called to testify] of the sufferings of Christ, as well as one who shares in the glory that is to be

revealed: <u>*shepherd and guide and protect the flock of God among you, exercising oversight not under compulsion, but voluntarily, according to the will of God; and not [motivated] for shameful gain, but with wholehearted enthusiasm;*</u> *not lording it over those assigned to your care [do not be arrogant or overbearing], but be examples [of Christian living] to the flock [set a pattern of integrity for your congregation]. And when the Chief Shepherd (Christ) appears, you will receive the [conqueror's] unfading crown of glory. Likewise, you younger men [of lesser rank and experience], be subject to your elders [seek their counsel]; and all of you, clothe yourselves with humility toward one another [tie on the servant's apron], for God is opposed to the proud [the disdainful, the presumptuous, and He defeats them], but He gives grace to the humble. Therefore, humble yourselves under the mighty hand of God [set aside self-righteous pride], so that He may exalt you [to a place of honor in His service] at the appropriate time"* – 1 Peter 5:1-6 Amplified Bible.

According to this passage, we see apostle Peter speaking to church leaders about the pattern and principle of leadership to the church of our Lord Jesus Christ.

First, we see him appealing to them as Fellow Elders. Peter started with an act of humility. Though he was an apostle with an apostolic authority, he humbled himself to the level of the church leaders where they are to instruct them. He began by saying: *"To the elders among you, I appeal as a fellow elder, a witness of Christ's sufferings and one who also will share in the glory to be revealed." -* 1 Peter 5:1.

Peter is urging them. He is exhorting and appealing to church leaders. "Appeal" (NIV), "exhort" (KJV, NRSV) is the Greek verb *parakaleō*. The basic meaning is "to call to one's side." Here, it means, "to urge strongly, appeal to, urge, exhort, encourage." In other contexts, it can mean, "request, implore, entreat" and "comfort, encourage, cheer up." Peter is earnest with his appeal to the church, but to fulfill this, he had to humble himself to address them.

As a leader, we must always humble ourselves to fulfill our leadership mandate, so that things are done according to the desire of the Lord to fulfill God's purpose for His Kingdom.

Again, Jesus Christ is our model and greatest example of humility. We are admonished in **Colossians 2:6,** to constantly walk in [union with] Him [reflecting His character in the things we do and say – living lives that will lead others into a right standing].

"Have this same attitude in yourselves which was in Christ Jesus [look to Him as your example in selfless humility], who, although He existed in the form and unchanging essence of God [as One with Him, possessing the fullness of all the divine attributes—the entire nature of deity], did not regard equality with God a thing to be grasped or asserted [as if He did not already possess it, or was afraid of losing it]; but emptied Himself

[without renouncing or diminishing His deity, but only temporarily giving up the outward expression of divine equality and His rightful dignity] by assuming the form of a bond-servant, and being made in the likeness of men [He became completely human but was without sin, being fully God and fully man]. After He was found in [terms of His] outward appearance as a man [for a divinely-appointed time], He humbled Himself [still further] by becoming obedient [to the Father] to the point of death, even death on a cross. For this reason also [because He obeyed and so completely humbled Himself], God has highly exalted Him and bestowed on Him the name which is above every name, so that at the name of Jesus [a]every knee shall bow [in submission], of those who are in heaven and on earth and under the earth, and that every tongue will confess and openly acknowledge that Jesus Christ is Lord (sovereign God), to the glory of God the Father" – Philippians 2:5-11 Amplified Bible.

Clearly, the character of Jesus Christ is humility; it reveals to us that humility is the secret to greatness and elevation in the Kingdom of God.

"Likewise, you younger men [of lesser rank and experience], be subject to your elders [seek their counsel]; and all of you, clothe yourselves with humility toward one another [tie on the servant's apron], for God is opposed to the proud [the disdainful, the presumptuous, and He defeats them], but He gives grace to the humble. Therefore, humble yourselves under the mighty hand of

God [set aside self-righteous pride], so that He may exalt you [to a place of honor in His service] at the appropriate time" – 1 Peter 5:5-6 Amplified Bible.

In conclusion:

"The plans and reflections of the heart belong to man, But the [wise] answer of the tongue is from the Lord. All the ways of a man are clean and innocent in his own eyes [and he may see nothing wrong with his actions], But the Lord weighs and examines the motives and intents [of the heart and knows the truth]. Commit your works to the Lord [submit and trust them to Him], And your plans will succeed [if you respond to His will and guidance]. A man's mind plans his way [as he journeys through life], But the Lord directs his steps and establishes them" - Proverbs 16:1-3; 9 Amplified Bible.

<u>**A good and effective leader will always seek God's direction in whatever he or she does**</u>. There is nothing more important in the life of a leader than to seek God's direction; not only for themselves, but also for the people they lead. A good leader seeks the Lord, commits his way to the Lord, and the Lord establishes his steps.

A good and effective leader is not puffed up or selfish. We have all encountered the know-it-all kind of leader. However, we clearly see through the Scripture from Proverbs 16:5 that, "Everyone who is arrogant in heart is an abomination to the Lord; he or she will not go unpunished." Therefore, it is very important that we humble ourselves to the Lord, so He can direct our paths, and make His will and plan known to us. In doing this, His will can be done here on earth, through us.

<u>Ministry Booking</u>

To Invite The Author To Speak At A Conference, A local Church or City, Please Contact Him At:

Apostle Emmanuel Echidime
New Life Global Church
948 William Booth Crescent,
Oshawa, Ontario L1G 7N4
Canada

Tel: (+1) 289 927 0232
Email: emma_echidime@yahoo.ca

Visit Us Online
@
www.newlifeglobalchurch.org